Children Are a Gift of God

DEBBIE KINGSTON BAKER

HARVEST HOUSE PUBLISHERS
Eugene, Oregon 97402

Children Are a Gift of God

Copyright © 1999 Harvest House Publishers
Eugene, Oregon 97402

ISBN 0-7369-0113-2

Arts Uniq'
P.O. Box 3085
Cookeville, TN 38502
800-223-5020

Design and production by Garborg Design Works, Minneapolis, Minnesota

Harvest House Publishers has made every effort to trace the ownership of all poems and quotes. In the event of a question arising from the use of a poem or quote, we regret any error made and will be pleased to make the necessary correction in future editions of this book.

Scripture quotations are taken from The Living Bible, Copyright © 1971 owned by assignment by Illinois Bank N.A. (as trustee). Used by permission of Tyndale House Publishers, Inc., Wheaton, Illinois 60189. All rights reserved; from the New American Standard Bible, © 1960, 1962, 1963, 1968, 1971, 1972, 1973, 1975, 1977 by The Lockman Foundation. Used by permission; from the Holy Bible, New International Version®, Copyright © 1973, 1978, 1984 by the International Bible Society. Used by permission of Zondervan Publishing House; and from the King James Version.

Printed in China.

99 00 01 02 03 04 05 06 07 08 /PP/ 10 9 8 7 6 5 4 3 2 1

Children are a gift of the Lord…they are His reward.
Happy is the man who has his quiver full of them.

THE BOOK OF PSALMS

3

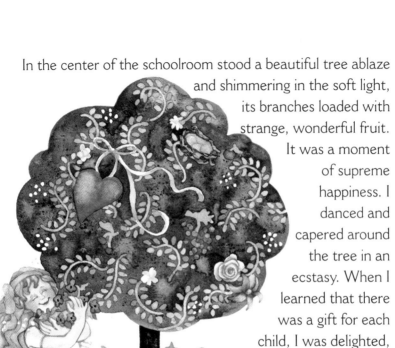

In the center of the schoolroom stood a beautiful tree ablaze and shimmering in the soft light, its branches loaded with strange, wonderful fruit. It was a moment of supreme happiness. I danced and capered around the tree in an ecstasy. When I learned that there was a gift for each child, I was delighted, and the kind people who had prepared the tree permitted me to hand the presents to the children.

HELEN KELLER

4

Little Girls

God made the little boys for fun, for rough and tumble times of play;
He made their little legs to run and race and scamper through the day.
He made them strong for climbing trees, He suited them for horns and drums,
And filled them full of revelries so they could be their father's chums.
But then He saw that gentle ways must also travel from above.
And so, through all our troubled days He sent us little girls to love.

He knew that earth would never do, unless a bit of Heaven it had.
Men needed eyes divinely blue to toil by day and still be glad.
A world where only men and boys made merry would in time grow stale,
And so He shared His Heavenly joys that faith in Him should never fail.
He sent us down a thousand charms, He decked our ways with golden curls
And laughing eyes and dimpled arms. He let us have His little girls.

They are the tenderest of His flowers, the little angels of His flock,
And we may keep and call them ours, until God's messenger shall knock.
They bring to us the gentleness and beauty that we sorely need;
They soothe us with each fond caress and strengthen us for every deed.
And happy should that mortal be whom God has trusted, through the years,
To guard a little girl and see that she is kept from pain and tears.

EDGAR GUEST

5

You made all the delicate, inner parts of my body, and knit them together in my mother's womb. Thank you for making me so wonderfully complex! It is amazing to think about. Your workmanship is marvelous—and how well I know it…. You saw me before I was born and scheduled each day of my life before I began to breathe. I will praise you because I am fearfully and wonderfully made.

THE BOOK OF PSALMS

6

Oh, the eagerness and freshness of youth!
How the boy enjoys his food,
his sleep, his sport, his
companions, his truant
days! His life is an
adventure, he is
widening his
outlook, he is
extending his
dominion, he
is conquering
his kingdom.
How cheap are
his pleasures, how
ready his enthusiasm!

JOHN BURROUGHS

7

'Tis a happy thing
To be the father of many sons.

WILLIAM SHAKESPEARE

8

Children are a sweet new blossom of humanity,
fresh fallen from God's own home, to flowers on earth.

MASSEY

9

Children have neither
past nor future…they
enjoy the present.

JEAN DE LA BRUYERE

10

Sell your books at
sellbackyourBook.com!
Go to sellbackyourBook.com
and get an instant price
quote. We even pay the
shipping - see what your old
books are worth today!

Inspected By: Raquel_Aguilar

00005832325354

0005832

5354 s

Oh, the joy of young ideas painted on the mind, in the warm, glowing colors fancy spreads on objects not yet known, when all is new and all is lovely.

HANNAH MORE

How beautiful is youth! How bright it gleams
With its illusions, aspirations, dreams!
Book of Beginnings, Story without End,
Each maid a heroine, and each man a friend!

HENRY WADSWORTH LONGFELLOW

It is not a slight thing when they, who
are so fresh from God, love us.

CHARLES DICKENS

13

Each child is created in the special
image and likeness of God for greater
things—to love and be loved.

The children bring us back to God; in eyes that dance and shine
Men read from day to day the proof of love and power divine;
for them are fathers brave and good and mothers fair and true,
For them is every cherished dream and every deed we do.

EDGAR GUEST

15

The Baby

Where did you come from, baby dear?
Out of the everywhere into the here.
Where did you get your eyes so blue?
Out of the sky as I came through.
What makes the light in them sparkle and spin?
Some of the starry spikes left in.
Where did you get that little tear?
I found it waiting when I got here.
What makes your forehead so smooth and high?
A soft hand stroked it as I went by.
What makes your cheek like a warm white rose?
I saw something better than anyone knows.

Whence that three-cornered smile of bliss?
Three angels gave me at once a kiss.
Where did you get this pearly ear?
God spoke, and it came out to hear.
Where did you get those arms and hands?
Love made itself into hooks and bands.
Feet, whence did you come, you darling things?
From the same box as the cherubs' wings.
How did they all just come to be you?
God thought about me and so I grew.
But how did you come to us, you dear?
God thought about you, and so I am here.

GEORGE MACDONALD

We find a delight in the beauty and happiness of children,
that makes the heart too big for the body.

RALPH WALDO EMERSON

…I am out of doors all the time, rowing, swimming, riding, and doing a multitude of other pleasant things. This morning I rode over twelve miles on my tandem! I rode on a rough road, and fell off three or four times, and am now awfully lame! But the weather and the scenery were so beautiful, and it was such fun to go scooting over the smoother part of the road, I didn't mind the mishaps in the least.

HELEN KELLER

Children are the hands
by which we take
hold of heaven.

HENRY WARD BEECHER

19

My lovely living boy,
My hope, my hap,
my love, my life, my joy.

DU BARTAS

They are idols of hearts and of households;
They are angels of God in disguise;
His sunlight still sleeps in their tresses,
His glory still gleams in their eyes;
Those truants from home and from Heaven
They have made me more manly and mild;
And I know now Jesus could liken
The kingdom of God to a child.

CHARLES M. DICKINSON

Beware that you do not look down upon a single one
of these children. For I tell you that in heaven their
angels have constant access to my Father.

THE BOOK OF MATTHEW

When the lessons and tasks are all ended,
And the school for the day is dismissed,
The little ones gather around me,
To bid me good-night and be kissed;
Oh, the little white arms that encircle
My neck in their tender embrace
Oh, the smiles that are halos of heaven,
Shedding sunshine of love on my face.

CHARLES M. DICKINSON

If there is anything that will endure
The eye of God, because it is still pure,
It is the spirit of a little child,
Fresh from His hand, and therefore undefiled.

R.H. STODDARD

One laugh of a child
will make the holiest
day more sacred still.

ROBERT INGERSOLL

24

Someone asked her if she liked to study.
"Yes," she replied, "but I like to play also, and
I feel sometimes as if I were a music box with
all the play shut up inside me."

HELEN KELLER

We need love's tender lesson taught
As only weakness can;
God hath His small interpreters;
The child must teach the man.

JOHN GREENLEAF WHITTIER

You are worried about seeing him spend his early years doing nothing. What! Is it nothing to be happy? Nothing to skip, play, and run around all day long? Never in his life will he be so busy again.

EMILE ROUSSEAU

I do not love him because he is good,
But because he is my little child.

28

A babe in the
house is a well-spring
of pleasure.

PROVERB

29

Child, you are
like a flower
So sweet and
pure and fair.

A garden of God
is our childhood,
each day
A festival with
laughter and play.

Micah J. Lebensohn

31

Children in a family are
like flowers in a
bouquet: There's
always one determined
to face in an opposite
direction from the way
the arranger desires.

MARCELENE COX

32

Nothing
fortuitous happens
in a child's world.
There are no
accidents.
Everything
is connected with
everything else and
everything can
be explained by
everything else…For
a young child every-
thing that happens
is a necessity.

JOHN BERGER

33

For children, childhood is
timeless. It's always the
present. Everything is in the
present tense. Of course, they
have memories. Of course,
time shifts a little for them
and Christmas comes round
in the end. But they don't feel
it. Today is what they feel,
and when they say "When I
grow up…" there's always an
edge of disbelief—how could
they ever be other than what
they are?

IAN MCEWAN

Even a minor event
in the life of a child
is an event of that
child's world and
thus a world event.

GASTON BACHELARD

She discovered with great
delight that one does not
love one's children just
because they are one's
children but because of
the friendship formed
while raising them.

GABRIEL GARCIA MARQUEZ

The plays of natural lively children are the infancy of art. Children live in a world of imagination and feeling. They invest the most insignificant object with any form they please, and see in it whatever they wish to see.

ADAM OEHLENSCHLAGER

The children bring us laughter, and the children bring us tears;
They string our joys, like jewels bright, upon the thread of years;
In every place where humans toil, in every dream and plan,
The laughter of the children shapes the destiny of man.

EDGAR GUEST

38

I love children. They do not prattle of
yesterday; their interests are all of
today and the tomorrows—I love children.

RICHARD MANSFIELD

One of my earliest recollections is of playing with books in my father's study, building houses and bridges of the big dictionaries and diaries, looking at pictures, pretending to read, and scribbling on blank pages whenever pen or pencil could be found…

LOUISA MAY ALCOTT

A Little Face

A little face to look at,
A little face to kiss;
Is there anything, I wonder,
That's half so sweet as this?

A little cheek to dimple
When smiles begin to grow,
A little mouth betraying
Which way the kisses go.

A slender little ringlet,
A rosy little ear,
A little chin to quiver
When falls the little tear.

A little hand so fragile,
All through the night to hold;
Two little feet so tender,
To tuck in from the cold.

Two eyes that watch the sunbeam
That with the shadow plays;
A darling little baby,
To kiss and love always.

BEAUTIFUL GEMS OF SENTIMENT

For this child I prayed; and the Lord hath given
me my petition which I asked of him.

THE BOOK OF 1 SAMUEL

41

The Children's Hour

I hear in the chamber above me
The patter of little feet,
The sound of a door that is opened,
And voices soft and sweet.
From my study I see in the lamplight,
Descending the broad hall stair,
Grave Alice, and laughing Allegra,
And Edith with golden hair.
A whisper, and then a silence:
Yet I know by their merry eyes
They are plotting and planning together
To take me by surprise.
They almost devour me with kisses,
Their arms about me entwine,
Till I think of the Bishop of Bingen
In his Mouse-Tower on the Rhine!

HENRY WADSWORTH LONGFELLOW

42

The Noon Recess

Oh! How the merry laugh and shout
Of happy little folks ring out
Upon the soft and balmy air
Sending sweet echoes everywhere!
Who but children can express
Half the delights of "Noon Recess"?
When from the books and study free,
Their little hearts o'erfull of glee,
No rule may meddle with the fun,
That's all their own—from twelve to one!

BEAUTIFUL GEMS OF SENTIMENT

43

I glanced at little
Jimmy, then glanced
at the other end
of the room where
a cot stood
to receive Rosie.

Soon, I thought,
I would have two
in here. I was
becoming rich.

JAMES HERRIOT

44

In God's Garden

Beauty is all around us
Placed here by God above;
Nowhere do we see this more
Than in the ones we love.

God sends little children
To remind us of the glory
Of the world and all its wonders
And each baby tells a story…

Beauty is all around us
Remember this and know
While the seeds are sown by God
It's up to us to grow!

ADAPTED FROM A POEM BY D. WILLIAM SMITH

45

Bed-Time

"The fire-flies are lighting the flowers to bed,"
I said to our little girl—tease,
As romping at dusk through the garden we sped;
And just then a soft little breeze
Bent down very gently each wee flower head,
And she with the gravest of airs,
Looked round at the stooped, breeze-bent flowers and said:
"And now are they saying their prayers?"

S. NORRIS

46

"When your children are young and growin'
up around ye—that's when it's best."

JAMES HERRIOT

As much as I converse with sages and heroes, they have very little of my love and admiration. I long for rural and domestic scenes, for the warbling of birds and the prattling of my children.

Childhood shows the man,
As morning shows the day.

JOHN MILTON

49

Around the child bent all three
Sweet Graces: Faith, Hope, Charity.

WALTER S. LANDOR

Behold the child, by nature's kindly law
Pleas'd with rattle, tickled with straw.

ALEXANDER POPE

Fortunately for children,
the uncertainties of the
present always give way
to the enchanted possibilities
of the future.

GELSEY KIRKLAND

Of all created things,
the loveliest and most
divine are children.

WILLIAM CANTON

Baby Feet

Tell me, what is half so sweet
As a baby's tiny feet,
Pink and dainty as can be,
Like a coral from the sea?
Talk of jewels strung in rows,
Gaze upon those little toes,
Fairer than a diadem
With the mother kissing them!
Little feet, so rich with charm,
May you never come to harm.
As I bend and proudly bow
Laughter out of every toe,
This I pray, that God above
Shall protect you with His love,
And shall guide those little feet
Safely down life's broader street.

EDGAR A. GUEST

Children live in a world directed by the senses as animals seem to do, and when the two meet, there arises an immediate bond, providing a sense of security, of pleasure, and of quiet understanding...Animals teach children friendship and loyalty, gentleness and kindness, and responsibility, too. They teach about birth and death and about the precious life to be experienced in between.

PAMELA PRINCE

My child, you hold the
whole of my heart in
your small hands.

The Family

The family is like a book—
The children are the leaves,
The parents are the covers
That protecting beauty gives.

At first the pages of the book
Are bland and purely fair
But Time soon writeth memories
And painteth pictures there.

ANONYMOUS

Children are apt to
live up to what you
believe of them.

LADY BIRD JOHNSON

58

For unflagging interest
and enjoyment, a
household of children,
if things go reasonably
well, certainly all other
forms of success and
achievement lose
their importance
by comparison.

THEODORE ROOSEVELT

59

Children Are

...poor men's riches.

JOHN RAY

...still the symbol of the eternal marriage between love and duty.

GEORGE ELLIOT

...the wisdom of the nation.

PROVERB

...our most valuable natural resource.

HERBERT HOOVER

...the key to paradise.

R. H. STODDARD

...a beam of sunlight from the Infinite
and Eternal, with possibilities of virtue
and vice—but as yet unstained.

LYMAN ABBOTT

...the best security for old age.

SHOLOM ASCH

...curly, dimpled lunatics.

RALPH WALDO EMERSON

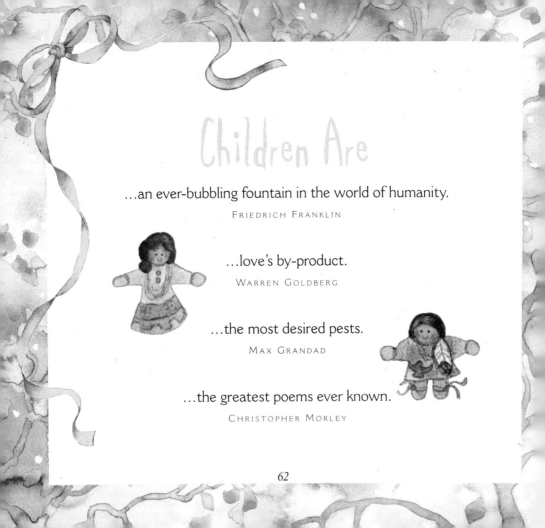

Children Are

...an ever-bubbling fountain in the world of humanity.

FRIEDRICH FRANKLIN

...love's by-product.

WARREN GOLDBERG

...the most desired pests.

MAX GRANDAD

...the greatest poems ever known.

CHRISTOPHER MORLEY

…an island of curiosity surrounded by
a sea of questions marks.

ANONYMOUS

…my jewels.

ROBERT BYRON

…those who always smell of bread and butter.

LORD BYRON

…of all people…the most imaginative. They abandon
themselves without reserve to every illusion.

THOMAS B. MACAULAY

…anchors that hold a mother to life.

SOPHOCLES

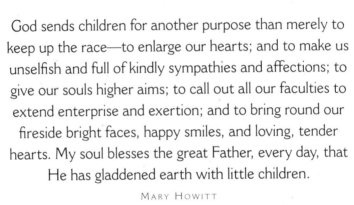

God sends children for another purpose than merely to keep up the race—to enlarge our hearts; and to make us unselfish and full of kindly sympathies and affections; to give our souls higher aims; to call out all our faculties to extend enterprise and exertion; and to bring round our fireside bright faces, happy smiles, and loving, tender hearts. My soul blesses the great Father, every day, that He has gladdened earth with little children.

MARY HOWITT